How to Invest in Gold and Silver

How learning the ways of investing in Gold and Silver can protect your wealth, diversify your portfolio and improve your profits

© Alan Dunwiddie
First Edition 2008

D1212147

Disclaimer

The Author has attempted to accurately represent the current laws and regulations applying to Gold and Silver investing, as well as the products and product providers described within this publication. However, please be aware that errors and omissions may occur and that this book is sold on the understanding that nothing contained within constitutes advice or inducement to invest in any way and that any statement or offer made cannot be relied upon as accurate or valid. You should thoroughly investigate and analyse your own personal situation and chosen investments or seek relevant professional advice before making any investment decisions of your own.

Copyright Alan Dunwiddie 2008
ISBN 978-87-92295-02-6

Published by Ad Publishing, Denmark.
http://www.adpublishing.eu

Front Cover Image : Sanja Gjenero at SXC Stock Photo
Back Cover Image : Grzegorz Kwiatkowski at SXC Stock Photo

CONTENTS

INTRODUCTION

Welcome to *How to Invest in Gold and Silver*. Against a backdrop of central banks selling their gold reserves, most notably the United Kingdom, which sold over half of the countries' gold reserves, 400 tonnes, at the almost rock bottom average price of $270 per ounce between 1999 and 2002, Gold has risen from an absolute low of $250 to the current price of $708 in 2007. Silver has risen from under $5 to $13 over the same period. Investors are starting to notice and are wondering why these prices are rising and how they can invest.

As you're reading this then you are probably interested, or are at least curious about investing in the precious metals of Gold and Silver. This book is an investigation into the reasons why you should consider including, most certainly, Gold and probably also Silver in your investment portfolio, followed by coverage of the many ways to do so, some of which you will have heard of and others you might not. The good news for most investors is that this book is intended for beginners. It will not dazzle you with pages of complex charts and options or derivatives trading methods, nor do you need to be an expert in mining companies and techniques, so one or more of the ways suggested will probably suit your style of investing.

Please note that where the book mentions actual fee costs or percentages for certain services, you should double check, as these often change with provider promotions and fee structure changes. The links to all sites mentioned in this publication are available at http://www.investgold.co.uk, and you can visit the links yourself to ascertain the current fees as part of calculating which investments will work best for you.

And now for the legal bit, this book is not directly inducing you to invest or not invest in any particular product, merely to identify opportunities to invest more cheaply, so that more of your money remains your own and secondly to identify possible areas of precious metals investment that are unknown to the majority of investors yet offer great scope to diversify your portfolio and improve your returns.

I hope you find the information contained within useful, stimulating and most of all, PROFITABLE.

Alan Dunwiddie,
Author.
http://www.investgold.co.uk

INFLATION
The Hidden Tax on Your Savings

You have probably never heard inflation called a tax before, but in the opinion of many experts that is exactly what is. To appreciate this you have to understand that no matter where you are living as you read this, your currency today is not backed by anything more than the "full faith of the government", otherwise known as a Fiat currency. As the government controls this currency, they have to ability to turn off and on the taps in creation of this currency, which they do in the main by setting Interest Rates, but scarily they could always just resort to cranking up the printing presses to pay off their debts, although this is an extreme situation. Assuming the setting of interest rates tool is used, a low interest rate stimulates the economy by encouraging more people to borrow more money and thus more money is issued by the lending bank, while a high interest rate discourages more borrowing and forces repayment of existing debt.

In case you are not quite clear, the last paragraph mentions the lending bank is issuing money. This means that subject to certain requirements, a lending bank is allowed to create money out of thin air when loaning money. It is a popular misconception that there has to be an equivalent deposit in the bank made by someone else. This is known as *fractional reserve banking*. Under this system, a bank is allowed to create loans for multiples of the deposits it holds. For example, consider a scenario where a bank has to retain only 20% of its deposits as a reserve. If you deposit £1,000 with a bank, then the bank may ultimately be allowed to loan out, say, £4,000 to potential borrowers. This means that there is extra £4,000 circulating in the economy, and that while you thought you were rich with your hard-earned £1,000, there are now other people with the exact same spending power as you, the only difference being that they produced that money via their own assumed future earnings. This is due to the cycle whereby borrowers spend their money on goods and services and the people receiving the money then deposit their new wealth in turn at a bank, who can then create even more loans against these new deposits. Now your original £1,000 deposit is being gradually diluted and it's spending power devalued by newly created currency.

Something you probably do realise about inflation is that it means increases in the cost of the every day items you need in order to live, but the real thing most people fail to realise is that these increases are often *decreases* in the value of your currency, usually due to the new currency creation schemes outlined. Your savings therefore should at least match the increase in inflation as of course the idea is that you will be able to cash them in at some point in future and enjoy at least the same benefit in spending them as you would from spending them right now.

When it comes to the official government inflation figures, these often understate true increases in the cost of living, due to the statistical reporting methods used. As the famous old adage goes, there are "lies, damned lies and statistics", and nowhere could this be truer than here. One method is to reduce the real price still further if the assumed quality of an item included in the basket of goods has gone up in quality. For example, a 2007 computer could be classified as ten times more powerful than a 1997 computer, and even though they have the same retail price of say, £1,000; the figures are adjusted downward due to the increased processing power: whether you really needed that extra processing power, or whether it is even possible to buy a 1997 specification computer is not considered. Another method is replacement, or substitution theory, where as a hypothetical example, say, if high quality beef rises in price, then it is assumed that many households will trade down to cheaper beef, or even some other type of meat.

Whether or not these are correct ways to measure price increases in anything is open to conjecture, but they do ultimately have the effect of making the official inflation figures lower.

Once upon a time, right up to the 1920s, most currencies were backed by gold, and you could walk into, say, the Bank of England and exchange your pound notes for the equivalent gold amount stated on them. These must have been happier times in many ways, since the value of your currency was fixed and the price of goods remained stable. This of course meant that your savings were virtually guaranteed to buy you a similar standard of living in the future as they would today.

For cash savings, low interest rates are of course bad news, but falsely low rates as controlled by a government maybe trying to win popularity with voters before an election rather than managing rates correctly, are bad news in another, more insidious way in that they cause more inflation and thus devalue your existing savings more rapidly.

As a share investor, inflation can lead to large rises in the profits stated by businesses, and at face value the obvious thing is to believe this is a good thing - in fact a dose of inflation is often presented as a good thing by governments. However, when businesses need to start working on recruiting new employees or buying new stock, they find that the prices for these items have started rising and their increased profitability was but a temporary phenomenon. In the worst cases, the raw materials to manufacture their product might actually now cost more than the price of their finished product and they could be driven out of business.

At the worst extremes, and historically this has happened many hundreds of times, a government destroys it's currency by inflation. Eventually, the holders of Pounds (Great Britain 1931), Marks (Germany 1921-23), Livres (France 1790s), or whatever all realise that their currency is being devalued and endeavour to get rid of it as quick as possible by buying whatever they think will hold its value instead. This has the effect of making the currency even more undesirable and worthless, which then becomes a downward spiral of which Zimbabwe is today's prime example.

A lesser documented effect of the inflation in Zimbabwe has been that the Zimbabwean stock market has in fact risen well in excess of the corresponding inflation, as holders of Zimbabwean dollars try to exchange their worthless currency for something of value such as shares in reliable businesses, often with safe overseas earnings or hard assets such as property or mining rights. The conclusion to draw from this is that in times of high inflation there are assets or businesses with pricing power that can protect you against the ravages of inflation.

The complex issue of inflation comes back to but one simple consideration for the astute investor to think about; Diversification. You probably already have some cash savings, and that is no bad thing since you will always have expenses to meet in your home country and are not so exposed to a stock market crash, plus if a government is honest about an inflation situation and raises interest rates dramatically then your savings have the benefit of receiving dramatic interest rates. But to be truly diversified and protected, you definitely should be holding some of your savings in the one item in world history which has always retained its purchasing power, and has always been viewed as a tradable item for goods and services, and that is gold.

GOLD AND SILVER AS MONEY

This book does not intend to go into great detail on this subject, as many, many pages have been written by true experts through the ages. Furthermore there are just too many historical examples of unsoundly managed fiat currency destroying the savings of ordinary people to cover here, not that your government really wants you to ever know about this. A Reading List is available at http://www.investgold.co.uk, so what follows is just a brief outline.

Gold (and silver) are traditionally the real units of currency upon which world trade is based. Historically they replaced all other forms of currency in civilisation such as sea-shells, stones, crops, etc. that were used as items for trade and barter because they are durable and not easy to replicate, so their future value is relatively assured. Gold especially has a reputation for not tarnishing or rusting, and is even resistant to some strong acids, meaning that as far as a medium of exchange goes there is nothing, quite literally, "as good as gold".

Paper money only came into being in the first place as a substitute for the practice of using physical gold and silver in transactions. What happened was that people deposited their gold with a bank, and then the bank would issue them with a promissory note, or notes for the value of their gold. People could then use their notes to buy goods and the person receiving the note knew they now owned the amount of precious metal stated on the note.

The real problems started occurring when people (normally banks, governments and forgers) began issuing extra notes backed by the same amount of precious metal, and, in 1971, the last historic link between gold and worldwide currency was removed by the USA, when they removed the link that 1 ounce of gold could be exchanged for 35 dollars and vice-versa. Up to this time, gold had a fixed value in terms of world trade.

It seems to be that every great nation in history begins with good intentions of a strong currency, since prior to the USA, Britain removed it's link to gold in the 1920s, after its own inflation problems due to the costs of paying for World War 1. The USA removed its link, at least in part, due to the cost of paying for the Vietnam War. During the 1960s, prior to removing the gold peg, they had built up to this by also removing from circulation all lower priced silver coinage, such as dimes and nickels, and minting new, cheaper alloy versions with the same face value.

Coincidentally (although perhaps not), the 1970s then saw rampant inflation, with gold finally reaching an all-time high of $850 dollars per ounce in 1980 and Silver peaking at $49 in 1980 after beginning the decade at under $2. Yes, you read that right, a 20-times plus return for holding what are probably the world's safest stores of value in your pocket. Could such times be repeated? Well, tie in today's current period of government-reported low inflation figures and indifference amongst a general population that has forgotten that gold and silver used to be the coins in our pockets to the mounting costs of wars in Afghanistan and Iraq. Sounds eerily similar, and therefore you might want to exchange some of your paper money "backed by the full faith of the Government" for some Gold, just in case. The book "Empire of Debt" is an interesting read in this respect.

It cannot be guaranteed that your Gold investments will increase 20-fold in terms of your local currency, but it is guaranteed, barring theft (governmental or otherwise) or such like that your ounce of gold will still be worth an ounce of gold, less any fees, when you choose to cash it in, and that it will still be tradable for an ounce of gold worth of goods such as food and clothing. This applies even if the Government goes bankrupt and the Dollar or Pound ever becomes a worthless piece of paper.

Just remember that whereas a government can print off as much currency as it likes, the amount of gold and silver can only increase by the amount that is mined yearly less the amount that is lost to manufacturing. In a bad year there could actually be less of this commodity in circulation than the previous year! This is especially true of silver, which in addition to its wealth value has a large number of manufacturing uses, such as in photography and electronics that deplete stocks.

It is also worth noting here that Gold is a purer representative of true wealth than silver. Although both metals have been heavily used throughout history as currency and to represent wealth, Gold has few uses apart from as money, whereas Silver is a heavily used industrial commodity and that can affect its price and desirability outside of any investment considerations. For example, some commentators are convinced that the rise of digital photography and the resultant downturn in traditional photography will result in a massive decrease in demand for silver, affecting the price as a result. This may or may not turn out to be true.

Apparently, the US government issues each of its pilots with 2 gold sovereigns to use for trade if they are ever shot down in enemy territory. Note that they don't issue them with a huge wad of paper dollars, which probably says something about the worldwide appeal of gold as a tradable item over even the most well-known internationally accepted national currency.

A more recent historical story of proof of Gold's real value came in 1933 at the height of the US depression. At this time an ounce of gold was exchangeable for $20 by government decree, but then the government made ownership of Gold illegal for US citizens and ordered the forcible confiscation of all privately held gold. Afterwards gold was revalued to $35 an ounce, although it remained illegal for a US citizen to own Gold right up until the 1970s. As you can probably see, if as a US citizen you held gold at this time you just got robbed of $15 for each ounce you originally held! The other side of the equation was that there were suddenly 75% more dollars in circulation, backed by the exact same underlying amount of gold. Possible Government confiscation is also something you might want to consider when choosing your investments and, as we'll see later, there are many new ways to hold your gold that were simply not possible for ordinary citizens all those years ago.

The US governments example from 1933 is merely another example of *debasing the coinage*, a practice that existed as far back as Roman times, and probably before that. In this scheme, if a coin was originally 90% gold, and the government needed some more coins in circulation, then they would re-melt the same coins as 80% gold, with the rest of copper or such like. This meant that they could then generate an extra number of coins to spend on their own schemes, such as costly foreign wars. Ultimately of course, the price of goods rose to reflect the debased coinage. Note that to prevent citizens from debasing the coinage by clipping the edges off themselves, coins often have a ribbed rim around the edge - a practice that continues to this day on many coins, gold or otherwise.

By now, you hopefully understand the difference between currency by governmental decree and hard currency. You may or may not also have realised that in reality, Gold, as the world's oldest currency, is the item of constant value, and that it is national currencies which decline or fall in value compared to the price of Gold. When you start looking at things this way, you begin to realise that when commentators talk about "the price of gold", this is a misnomer and perhaps a truer title would be "the value of the national currency", or such like.

Furthermore, when you link this fact with the chapter on Inflation, you begin to realise that another advantage of inflation for governments is that they are able to collect *Capital Gains Taxes* on illusory profits made by investors. As an example, if a national currency falls in value, by, say half, over a period of time and the value of your investment doubles in that same time then it might look good on paper, but the reality is no more than the financial equivalent of standing still.

GOLD CONSPIRACIES

Following on from the previous two chapters, you have probably derived certain conclusions about the vested interests of various parties in keeping the price of gold and silver low in relation to national currencies, or, conversely, to make the value of national currencies, not backed by anything, appear to be of some value. But, in the words of Francis Urquhart, fictional UK Prime Minister in the top BBC Drama, "House of Cards";

"….*you* might think that, but I couldn't possibly comment".

However, coincidentally enough, the UK itself was home to a curious happening worthy of note in the field of Gold, when, in 1999 it was decided to sell off over half the nations' gold reserves, some 400 tonnes. At the time, Gold was at the end of a major 20-year bear market, and the price was at an all-time low, a price last seen in the 1970s. The Bank of England, custodian of the countries' Gold reserves insists that it was never consulted in the decision, and some leaks in fact suggest that many of their staff vigorously opposed the move. They claim that the decision was made by Her Majesty's Treasury, and them alone. At the time, the Chancellor of the Exchequer was a Mr. Gordon "Golden" Brown, who has subsequently become Prime Minister.

Even worse, the huge Gold sales and auctions were publicly announced well in advance, thus giving gold dealers the chance to prepare for the glut of gold that was about to be released onto the market, and force the price down still further as a result. Normal strategy is to keep intended government gold sales quiet, then simply conduct the sales on the open market, obtaining the best prices possible, then announce the results afterwards.

Why might a government decide to sell off one of the main assets of its people at the lowest price possible? Well, you might be surprised to hear that there are various Gold conspiracists, many of them persons of note in the financial world, who earnestly believe that the price of gold versus national currencies is often managed in this way and who have a field day with this sort of thing. In this case, there are rumours and accusations that the gold was sold to prevent top Hedge Funds who had gambled on the price of Gold from going bust and destroying the worldwide economy, among others.

This is just one story of many that the Gold conspiracists believe is occurring in our worldwide economy, and that, one day, people may realise, like Germans did in 1921-23, that their money is "not worth the paper it's printed on". This book has no specific comment to make on any aspect of this case, except that 1999-2002 has subsequently been proved to have been exactly the right time to start buying Gold, not selling it; in fact, the value of the Gold sold by the UK has risen by over *five billion dollars* since that time. If you want to know more about this story, and other alleged conspiracy theories behind

Gold, then please visit http://www.gata.org, home of the Gold Anti-Trust action committee (GATA), a well-known organisation, who believe that the value of Gold is being secretly manipulated.

Another major concern of note for GATA is the fact that of the Gold reserves still held by major nations, much of it has been loaned out. In this case, the custodians of the gold, the central banks loan out their gold to a third party, who pays an agreed interest for loan of the gold. This third party can then do whatever they like with the gold, including selling it on. This is a likely deal if the borrower wanted to gamble on the price of Gold falling, for example. The original agreement is, of course, that an equivalent amount of gold will one day be returned to the central bank. But no audits have ever been carried out to find out how much physical Gold the central banks really hold, and how much has been loaned out. If there was ever a major crisis and the central banks want their Gold back, what is the likelihood that all of it will be returned, or be available to be returned by the borrowing parties? And what will be the effect on the price of Gold if these borrowers are forced to all at once buy fresh Gold to honour their promises? For example, the USA remains the nation that reports the largest Gold reserves in the world, but in the absence of concrete evidence, many commentators are dubious how much Gold the USA still really has in safe-keeping.

Silver is not without its own conspiracy theories. As a much used industrial commodity, it is in the best interests of many to keep the price as low as possible for as long as possible. It is thought by many commentators that the price has been manipulated for many years to be artificially low, and is in no way representative of how much Silver exists in physical form. For example, on COMEX, the main New York USA exchange for trading silver, there may be more short sales than there is silver to back them up. Again, if this is true, then imagine what would happen if those sellers were all forced to buy silver on the open market to meet their promises? And more importantly, would they even be able to? In the USA, there is even a *Silver Users Association*, representing the viewpoint of businesses that consume silver, and lobbying government when necessary to protect those interests. They successfully managed to delay, but not stop, the introduction of the first ever Silver investment fund, the Barclays iShares Silver ETF in 2006 (for an explanation of ETFs, see the *Exchange-Traded Funds* chapter).

There are certainly plenty of interesting stories of intrigue and note out there on this subject, and there are many who think that if there is an asset your government preferred you didn't own, well then, it is probably a major asset you *should* consider owning.

So, hopefully, faced with all of this knowledge, you are now fired up to at least consider diversifying some of your savings into precious metals, so let's look at the main methods available and the major disadvantages of each.

GOLD AND SILVER COINS

As most of the major nations were part of the Gold Standard which ended after World War 1 (1918), there are a huge variety of Gold Coins available to collectors and Gold investors.

These coins were produced by many different nations and can be in high demand with collectors; hence their value can vary over and above that of the underlying gold metal. The great thing for anyone buying these kind of gold coins, not just numismatists (coin collectors), is the fact of holding a piece of real history, of everlasting value, in your hand.

In addition, many gold producing countries like South Africa, Australia and Canada still produce new gold and silver coins of standard weights.

Gold coins in particular are rarely made from solid (or 24 carat) Gold. This is because gold is, despite its value and inert properties, a soft metal that can scratch or damage fairly easily. To increase the wear of coins, they were traditionally mixed in an alloy with another metal such as copper. For example, Gold sovereigns are 90% Gold.

The same goes for silver coins as with gold, although as Silver is of much lower value these normally constituted the smaller value coins in circulation. These are even easier to find than Gold Coins and remained in use for a much longer period. For example, if you have any old British Shillings dated prior to 1947 these contain silver instead of Nickel.

The great thing about silver coins is that they can often be bought for less than the silver value weight of the coins. This is often true of the base, low value coins of yesteryear where many millions were originally minted.

Advantages of Gold and Silver Coins

- As standard coins, they are of easily recognisable, documented weight and value.
- They are small, portable forms of wealth easily carried on your person in a time of crisis.
- Physical possession of Gold and Silver coins is the ultimate way of retaining your wealth. Only theft (governmental or otherwise) can take your wealth from you.
- Gold and <u>Old</u> Silver coins in the European Union do not attract VAT.
- Good news for British investors is that expert opinion is that the sale of Gold Sovereigns does not attract Capital Gains Tax (CGT) either. This is not something the Inland Revenue would be keen to advertise, but is due to the fact that Sovereigns have a face value of One Pound and therefore still qualify as currency of the realm. They therefore hold huge advantages for British Investors. The same may be true for buying face value gold coinage in the currency of whatever country you live

in, although you need to check these rules for yourself.

Disadvantages of Gold and Silver Coins

- Premiums are often higher than other forms of investment outlined later
- Physical possession could make you a target for theft so remember to find a safe hiding place
- New Silver coins can attract VAT in the European Union, and if so should be avoided
- When you come to sell, it might be hard to find a willing buyer at close to the underlying metal price – your coin dealer will offer a similar percentage under the gold price to what he charged you over the gold price, unless your coins are also desirable to collectors.

In summary, visit a reputable coin dealer to make sure you are getting coins that are worth the money, and that you do not pay too much over the underlying value of the metal in the coin. Tell him you are mainly interested in the metal value and not the numismatic element. In this respect, British Sovereigns and South African Krugerrands often seem to have fairly low percentage premiums above the gold value and are universally recognised coins.

Your own government may sometimes also bring out special "limited edition" coin sales that might even include gold bullion coins. These should normally be avoided because the premiums above the underlying metal prices are usually very high. You can often visit coin dealers directly later to purchase the same, or similar coins at much lower premiums. You can always use the internet to check if they are a good deal against published coin dealer prices.

EBay and other auction sites are not particularly recommended since you have no way of verifying a sellers' claim until after you have handed your money over. The prices attained on the internet right now also seem rather high considering the additional risks of not having seen or examined the items beforehand and possible postal loss.

Conversely, EBay might turn out to be a good place to sell your coins if there is ever a crisis in the future and Gold is suddenly in great demand again, because you are able to advertise to a worldwide audience at very low cost.

It is also possible to buy coins from many specialist dealers on the internet, but remember to check out the commissions you'll be paying, insured postage costs and also whether you'll be liable for customs fees on delivery.

Finally, remember what was said earlier, that the US air force issues all of its pilots with 2 gold sovereigns to use in trade if they are shot down. This surely tells us something about the value of owning gold coins in a time of crisis.

GOLD AND SILVER BARS

These have a lot of the advantages and disadvantages of Coins, such as physically owning the metal. Bars are made in various sizes and can be as convenient to own as the coins, but there are some other factors to consider.

Advantages of Gold and Silver Bars

- Bullion bars are usually available for really low premiums above the gold or silver price.
- Bullion bars can be easily identified and valued, as they are usually hallmarked
- Gold bars do not attract VAT in the EU.

Disadvantages of Gold and Silver Bars

- Silver bars do attract VAT in the EU. No EU investor should consider investing in silver bars because of this rule.
- A bullion bar cannot be split into smaller units for trading.

The same dealer who can sell you coins can normally also sell bullion bars on the same basis. It is also possible to buy bullion bars from many specialist dealers on the internet, but remember to check out the commissions you'll be paying, insured postage costs and also whether you'll be liable for customs fees on delivery.

JEWELLERY

Historically, the wearing of jewellery probably comes to a large extent from the need to carry your stored wealth with you, be it in the form of rings, necklaces or whatever.

Now, since jewellery is the precious metal item most advertised as being of a certain number of *carats*, this seems like a good time to explain what a carat is. It is a measure of Gold purity, between 1 and 24, where 24 is the highest quality purity. So, if an item is 24 carat gold, it is over 99% Gold, about as close to pure gold as it is possible to get. If it is 18-carat, it is 75%, 12-carat means 50%, and 9-carat means 37.5% Gold. Many coins are, like Gold sovereigns for example, 90% gold and therefore 22-carat, and hence the different gold hues associated with the different levels of purity, as the rest is made up of base metals. What this means in reality is that if you, have for example, a 9-carat gold ring, you should weigh it then multiply the weight by 0.375 to obtain the weight of gold it contains. You can then multiply this by the daily price for Gold given in most newspapers to get the approximate value of the ring if you were to sell it today. You might be shocked at how little some of your favourite items are underlyingly worth compared to how much you paid for them.

As silver is much less valuable, silver items are normally of a much higher purity, although pure silver is still often too soft for jewellery and thus jewellery is normally made of silver alloys like *Sterling Silver*. Sterling Silver is 92.5% silver, with the balance made up of something like copper to increase the resilience.

Most jewellery in Europe and the USA is worth a lot less than the retail prices in the shops. If gold and silver even came into demand again, you could probably imagine customers at retail stores no longer taking sales assistants at face value when they say such and such item is "18-carat", for example, and asking them detailed questions about how much it weighs and what the precious metal content actually is.

Other regions such as the Middle East and India place far more emphasis on the actual precious metals value of jewellery. It is only conjecture, but perhaps they have more recent examples of financial crises in their histories, which makes them more aware of the inherent value of such items, and Dubai, for example, is said by some to be a good place to buy high quality gold jewellery at fairly small premiums above the underlying precious metal value.

Advantages of Jewellery

- Jewellery can certainly be the most aesthetically pleasing precious metal option.
- Personal possession of precious metal
- Can be carried upon your person in times of extreme crisis
- Probably safe from government confiscation under all but the most extreme circumstances

Disadvantages of Jewellery

- Large mark-ups above the metal price for extra manufacture and retail costs
- Unlike coins and bars, they are not easily identifiable storage forms of value. Only an expert can probably identify the quality and value of a given gold ring, for example.

Jewellery is therefore not recommended beyond its emotional value to the owner, but a gold wedding ring is a handy, if you excuse the pun, final backup resource to own in a time of extreme crisis.

OTHER GOLD AND SILVER ITEMS

Here it is worth mentioning other types of Gold and Silver items that people can accumulate. This could be souvenir gold nuggets, gold teeth or, especially in the case of silver, aesthetically pleasing items such as silver tea sets or cutlery that have been passed down through the generations.

While these may often have a value well in excess of the metal value, the point is that they are worth at least the value of the metal they are manufactured from.

Aside from the lack of portability of large items, all the advantages and disadvantages of jewellery apply, and if you do have any such items in the house, it may be well worth weighing them to find out their base metal value for starters.

It is sometimes possible to buy damaged or worn scrap items at well below the value of the metal at junk sales and the like. These can often be a good, cheap way of gaining some precious metals exposure at a fair price.

STORING YOUR GOLD AND SILVER SAFELY

It may be possible for you to visit your bank and say you wish to purchase gold or silver and they can arrange a deal. But watch the terms of the deal closely.

It may also be possible for your bank to arrange storage of any physical gold you already own in a Safe deposit box.

When it comes to Gold storage there are two forms of ownership to take into account and the difference between these two forms of ownership is vital, as they could mean the difference between something and nothing in the event of a crisis.

Allocated Storage
The gold belongs to you and the bank is only acting as an agent holding it on your behalf. If you really want your bank to manage a gold investment for you, then it needs to be held like this because it's the only way you are protected if the bank collapses.

Unallocated Storage
You only bought a share in the banks' gold. This is not desirable at all since the bank still has the rights over the gold and you are only another creditor of the bank. The bank can freely sell that gold in the event of an emer-

gency to pay its creditors, including you (join the queue!).

Advantages of Bank Storage

- Could be a fair deal, depending on the fees.
- Depending on what the future holds, it could be safer than storing them at your home

Disadvantages of Bank Storage

- A bank's primary business nowadays is the issuing of currency, not managing gold. They will charge yearly storage fees for holding your gold.
- In 1933, when the USA confiscated all the nations' gold, where was the first place they looked? That's right, in bank safety deposit boxes. It was even made illegal to open a bank safety deposit box without a warden present.
- If your gold is unallocated, then a bank collapse is a disaster, but even if it's not, would you trust an organisation in this state to safely guard your gold? Consider further that bank collapses normally accompany the inflationary situations that make gold a desirable asset to own.

The alternative is a storage option of your own choice, be it a hidden safe in your home, or even a hole in the ground. The large number of archaeological gold and silver hoards dating from hundreds or thousands of years ago that are found are probably evidence of the crises our ancestors had to face and the lengths they had to go to guard their wealth.

Fortunately, compared to our ancestors, we now have many more options to safeguard our wealth by linking at least some of our investments to gold and silver. These investments can often protect your wealth outside of your local government jurisdiction, which can be another useful factor in their favour. So we will now be looking at paper and electronic forms of gold and silver.

INVESTMENT FUNDS AND MINING STOCKS

If you have a financial advisor advising you on your investments and you mentioned a gold/silver angle, he would likeliest mention investing in a Gold or Natural Resources fund, but you need to be aware that this usually really means a fund investing in mining companies. Merrill Lynch Gold Unit Trust, for example, has magnificent performance figures over prior years, but much of this fund is invested in gold mining companies and not gold itself. This introduces many extra variables into the game, as well as the higher fund management fees that you will be paying.

To minimise these fees you could then decide to invest directly into mining stocks listed on the stock market yourself, and as the two investment forms are very similar, we will consider them together.

Well, in addition to worrying about the price of the underlying commodity, you have to ask the same business questions you would ask of any other corporation, e.g. is the company well-run? Are the countries in which the mines operate free and open or could the mines be confiscated? Is the mine environmentally conscious or are campaigners trying to get it closed down?

Yes, if you pick the right mining companies who discover huge reserves of gold or silver, then the price of these stocks will rise dramatically in excess of underlying commodity prices, but the simple fact to remember is that you are investing in stocks. As famous author Mark Twain once allegedly commented, "A mine is a hole in the ground with a liar at the top". It is possible to make huge profits in mining companies but you really need to do your homework.

Another thing to be aware of when investing stocks, especially gold stocks, is something called "production hedging". In practice, this means the selling of future mining production that has not yet being dug out of the mine, at a price acceptable to both parties, based on today's gold price.

In a falling gold price market, this could be a spectacularly profitable decision, but in a rising gold price market, a really bad business decision has been made because you are forced to sell your production at yesterdays much lower price. The key thing to realise is that this is another business factor that could affect your investment value. The solution? Always look for "unhedged" mining companies.

On the Stock Market, small mining companies in particular also often suffer from wide bid-offer spreads. In case you're not sure what the bid-offer spread is, this is when a share price is listed in the newspaper as being, say, 9p per share, but when you come to buy the price is 9.25p, and when you come to sell you are offered 8.75p. It occurs because the Market Maker is buying and selling these shares, making a profit by quoting a lower price to those wanting to sell their shares to him, and a higher price to those wanting to buy from him.

The bid/offer spread is one of the least understood parts of investing and hence one of the sneakiest ways for you to lose money without realising it. Only buy or sell when the bid/offer spread is tight - IE there is not much percentage difference between the selling price and buying price because then you know you are getting a fair deal. It is not uncommon to see shares (especially penny mining shares) listed at, say, 1.25p to sell and 2.5p to buy. This is a disaster transaction to be avoided at all costs - the share needs to double for you to get your money back and that doesn't even include other fees.

If you do fancy investing in mining stocks, then there are plenty of experts out there who produce newsletters with investing recommendations and who have proven successful track records along with great knowledge on the mining nuances of terms such as "provable resources" and the cost calculations involved in getting ore out of the ground and processed. So, if you are interested, then you should do some research yourself to find a newsletter that suits you and ride on the back of one these heavyweights.

The one caveat to this would be to consider investing in a miner such as the world's largest mining company, BHP Billiton. Large mining companies are hugely diversified operations with many streams of income from various commodities (even a gold mining company will produce silver and copper as by-products) and various mines throughout the world, so are not so affected by one bad decision or unforeseen circumstance in any one area. Okay, performance is unlikely to be so heart stopping as it would be with a small miner either, but it depends on your own investing aims.

Mining stocks are listed on many stock exchanges throughout the world, especially the USA, Australia, Canada, South Africa and, more latterly, the London AIM (Alternative Investment Market).

Advantages of Gold Mining Stocks

- Direct investing into mining companies gives you geared returns on the gold price increase. For example, if a miner makes $20 profit per ounce when gold is priced at $600, all other things being equal, he will make $40 profit per ounce if gold rises to $620. What other business can double profits like that?
- Mining companies could discover new reserves that boost company value too
- Investment funds are very diversified and give you more diversified coverage than you could ever attain investing on your own account
- Investing in foreign-listed gold mining stocks can put your wealth outside of local government jurisdiction

Disadvantages of Gold Mining Stocks

- The geared returns can work both ways – a fall in mineral prices can wipe out profitability altogether.
- Mining companies are subject to business or political variances outside of gold and silver prices.
- Direct investment into one or two companies does not give you a very diversified portfolio
- Small mining companies can be very illiquid to trade on world markets

There is one more way of accessing mining stocks, and that is through Exchange Traded Funds (ETFs) which are explained in the following chapter.

EXCHANGE-TRADED FUNDS

Exchange-Traded Funds, or ETFs are the new kid on the block, combining the pooled investment potential of Unit Trusts with much lower fees. They are listed on the stock market and as such are tradable in the same way as ordinary shares.

From a Stocks and Shares point of view, ETFs are exciting because they have the potential to offer a much broader range of investments. Already you can invest in various hitherto unavailable indexes directly, such as Chinese or Korean stock indexes, but the great thing is that there are now even opportunities to invest in commodities such as gold and silver. This has the potential to diversify or switch your portfolio more broadly than you could ever have done so in the past.

If you have a financial advisor, then depending on the type of financial advisor you use, they may not recommend or know about ETFs simply because they do not pay enough, if any, commission. This fact alone should tell you what a comparatively good deal ETFs are.

There are two ETF types of interest to Gold and Silver investments, and in both cases you can buy shares in the ETF itself through the stock market and join the party.

Some of these ETFs are simply tracking the gold or silver price. There are several Gold ETFs and at least one Silver ETF of this type you can invest in. You can check out ETF Securities, Barclay's iShares or Lyxor Gold, to name a few. Yearly fees are normally low. The funds either invest in the metals and store it in a vault or invest on the metals futures markets. Popular preference is for those funds that store the metal in a vault because your investment is more closely matched to the actual metal.

Other ETFs are simply buying a basket all of the mining stocks listed on a given stock market. These have the dual advantage of allowing investing in mining companies and achieving greater diversification than investing alone could ever do. Some of the ETFs you could consider include AMEX Gold Bugs and iShares CDN Gold, both listed in the USA.

At this point, you should consider the importance of looking for the cheapest online broker when investing, and in this respect, for those in the UK or EU, the UK-based broker Selftrade is worthy of consideration - their commission per deal is £12.50, which is not in itself the cheapest but they do have a price improvement promise which often seems to undercut the official bid/offer spread. Their accounts are available to non-UK residents who pass their ID requirements, and at time of writing this you can email selftrade@investgold.co.uk and you will get a £50 bonus for opening an account when recommended. It is guaranteed that your email address will remain confidential and not be passed on to any other parties or used for marketing purposes.

And if you live in the UK and want to invest through your tax-free ISA (Individual Savings Account) or SIPP (Self-invested Pension Plan), then Selftrade is also currently offering to rebate transfer fees up to £100 if you transfer your plan(s) to them and the same deal above about emailing <u>selftrade@investgold.co.uk</u> and getting a £50 bonus applies. It is guaranteed that your email address will remain confidential and not be passed on to any other parties or used for marketing purposes.

Advantages of ETFs

- The costs are also much lower then comparable Unit trusts. For example, Merrill Gold Unit Trust has, at time of writing, an initial charge of 5% and an annual charge of 1.75%. A near-equivalent ETF has an annual charge of 0.5% and the normal costs associated with purchase of a stock on the stock market.
- For UK investors, ETFs, unlike shares do not attract stamp duty
- Gold and Silver ETFs are passive tracker investments in the main so performance will almost match the equivalent index
- You do not have any personal storage costs to pay, and the pooled storage cost among all investors will be a lot cheaper
- For European Union investors, Silver ETFs are a way of legally owning Silver bullion without paying VAT

Disadvantages of ETFs

- Smaller ETFs are very illiquid and it can sometimes be difficult to get an on-line quote
- ETFs tend to be passive tracker investments in the main so performance will almost match the equivalent index – yes, this was also down as an advantage and in the main it probably is, but some may think you can do better by direct investing in mining stocks or spread betting.
- The Metals are not physically in your possession should you need the money quickly.

Overall, ETFs definitely have a place in a diversified Metals portfolio, especially for UK investors who can invest using their tax-free ISA allowance. This is covered more in the book *Successful Tax-Free ISA Investing* by the same author.

SPREAD BETTING

Here you are opening an account with a gambling website and wagering on whether the price of your chosen commodity will rise or fall in a given timescale. Bets are normally places at a price per unit, and that price per unit is multiplied by the units you win by or lose by to calculate your profit or loss on the wager.

Advantages of Spread Betting

- In many countries, gambling is classified as a leisure activity and thus profits or losses are not taxable transactions. This could be a great benefit.
- There are none of the physical costs associated with ownership of the metal.
- Spread Betting could allow you to play short term movements in the metals pricing markets to your advantage. For example, you could buy and sell on the same day with low transaction costs.

Disadvantages of Spread Betting

- Your Investment is quite far removed from owning physical gold. In the event of a severe crisis where you need money on hand right now, this could be a problem.
- You need to learn about and understand the vagaries and rules of spread betting, aside from any knowledge you may have about gold or silver.
- Your bets are normally placed at a unit per point loss or profit. E.g. £5 for every cent gold falls or rises. If a bet goes against you big time, you may lose a lot more than you originally invested.

If you are still interested then you could check out IG Index or Cantor, among the many companies out there offering this service, but before you begin investing serious money in spreadbetting, you could find out whether it suits your style by taking advantage of one of the offers available where you test the systems by either trading for free using imaginary funds, or trading at only, say, 1 pence per point.

THE FUTURES MARKET

Gold and silver are traded on the futures markets like any other commodity, with forward delivery dates and pricing based on what the majority investors expect gold to be at that time.

In case you're not sure what futures are, this is the market where a farmer or miner agrees to sell his forthcoming production at a certain price, to be delivered on a certain date. This contract can then be sold and resold by any number of investors. Whoever is holding the contract on the final delivery date is expected to take possession of the commodity in question. As an investor, you wouldn't be interested in the delivery, just in trading the contract on for profit prior to the delivery date.

Advantages of the Futures Market

- Could allow you to play short term movements in the metals pricing markets to your advantage.
- There are none of the physical costs associated with ownership of the metal.
- A lot of futures brokers allow you to invest "on margin", which means that you can put down, say, £500 and invest up to £10,000. If a bet goes your way big time, you can make an awful lot of money.

Disadvantages of the Futures Market

- Your Investment is removed from owning physical gold. In the event of a severe crisis where you need money on hand right now, or the futures market closes for some reason, this could be a problem.
- You need to learn about and understand the vagaries and rules of how the futures markets work, aside from any knowledge you may have about gold or silver.
- A lot of futures brokers allow you to invest "on margin", which means that you can put down, say, £500 and invest up to £10,000. If a bet goes against you big time, you may lose a lot more than you originally invested.

There are many companies out there offering this service. Interactive Brokers is one internet-based one that offers full online trading facilities at a reasonable price.

DERIVATIVES

Here's where you can move into really esoteric investments.

If you know a bit about the stock market then you may
have heard of things like Options or Contracts for Difference (CFDs). It is possible to play the same moves on
Gold and Silver mining stocks or commodity prices in
the same way as it is possible to do on other asset classes.

These are called derivatives, because they are investment
markets derived from the underlying asset prices, be it
stock or commodity prices.

Advantages of Derivatives

- Could allow you to play short term movements in
  the metals pricing markets to your advantage.
- There are none of the physical costs associated
  with ownership of the metal.
- Options and derivatives are a geared play on an
  asset class movement. A small price move in your
  favour can multiply the value of your original investment many times over.

Disadvantages of Derivatives

- Your Investment is removed from owning physical gold. In the event of a severe crisis where you need money on hand right now, or the market closes for some reason, this could be a problem.
- You need to learn about and understand the vagaries and rules of how the markets work, aside from any knowledge you may have about gold or silver.
- Options and derivatives are normally a geared play on an asset class movement. Even a small move against you can destroy your original investment and leave you owing a lot more besides.

To summarise, derivatives may not be the best investing move for the introductory gold and silver investors this book is intended for. They require a lot of specialist knowledge and if you really want to find out more about options trading, and other related investment classes, then it is recommended that you read specialist literature and become comfortable with the concepts before risking any of your investment capital.

PERTH MINT CERTIFICATES

Perth Mint certificates are a new way of buying title to Australian Gold through certificates. The Perth Mint has existed since 1899 and is backed by the State government of Western Australia.

They offer both Allocated and Unallocated storage. These two options were described in the section on Gold Storage, and you may remember that Allocated is the recommended option. Allocated attracts a fabrication and storage fee in this case, but unallocated does not.

These can only be bought through official brokers of Perth Mint certificates. Research as of 2006 shows that they do not all charge the same fees, so it is recommended you visit the list of recommended brokers on their website and investigate thoroughly. For example, *Pacific Capital* quoted a lesser price than *Gold and Silver Investments*, even though the latter was a more local dealer for the author (UK and Ireland). You should be able to use any dealer you wish.

There are a lot of ID requirements for people wishing to invest in Perth Mint Certificates, including a potential need for notarised documents from a lawyer, so this might be something else you need to consider in your investing plans.

Advantages of Perth Mint Certificates

- Western Government-backed guarantee
- For the likes of US or European investors, for example, your Investment lies far away from local government jurisdiction
- Low Fees
- Offers allocated storage
- No VAT on Silver purchases for EU buyers

Disadvantages of Perth Mint Certificates

- High initial investment required (10,000 US$)
- Can only cash in the bonds in large units
- Only a limited number of brokers retail this service
- The service is paper-based and not internet based, so it may take a while to get your money back when you decide to cash in, and, unless you live in Perth, your metals could be very hard to access in a time of crisis

Conclusion is that those looking to squirrel away a large sum for long-term investment purposes may find these the best investing option. Their Australian location may also appeal to those subject to other government jurisdictions. The Perth Mint does in fact advertise that no taxes are payable on purchases or sales of precious metals in Australia, and that Australia allows free movement of precious metals in and out of Australia.

Perth Mint also have a Gold-tracking product similar to an ETF listed on the Australian Stock Exchange (code ZAUWBA), but in this case it is traded as a warrant. In case you are not aware, a *Warrant* is a type of *derivative*, and is actually the right to buy a product (usually shares in a company), within a given time period, at a certain price. In this case, however, each warrant gives the right to buy 1 ounce of fine gold from Gold Corporation, the owners of the Perth Mint, and can be exercised by the holder at any time up 31st December 2013.

ELECTRONIC GOLD AND SILVER

Electronic gold, and more lately electronic silver, is a superb idea that could only ever have been made possible by the internet. The theory is that you exchange your money with an internet-based organisation that then gives you an account containing an equivalent number of gold units. These gold units are your bank account and theoretically backed by an equivalent amount of gold held on storage somewhere.

The gold units you hold can be held or exchanged for services bought over the internet. If you hold the units, you will have to pay a storage fee for your gold, although as with ETFs this will be less than trying to go it alone. Normally, storage will also be *Allocated*, and you might remember that this is the preferred storage option, since it means there is some real metal out there that belongs to you.

You are normally free to exchange your gold back into a variety of national currencies at any time, at the prevailing gold exchange rate less a small fee, either fixed or a percentage. Some providers allow you to retain your national currency with them; others will pay it back to you. The ease with which you are able to withdraw your currency and receive it back in your bank account is also something else you may need to consider.

The Major Fees to Consider are:-

Storage Cost
Usually quoted monthly as a percentage, or a fixed amount. The fixed amount is normally the best deal for larger holdings.

Buy Transaction Cost
Same as with coins, there will be a bid-offer spread, where you pay, say, 2% over spot price to buy. Also remember to investigate whether there will be any other fees applicable to your situation, for example, personal bank fees if you live in Norway and the digital currency provider only accepts dollars.

Sell Transaction Cost
Just the same as with coins, there will be a bid-offer spread where you receive, say, 2% under spot price when you sell. Also remember to investigate whether there will be any other fees applicable to your situation, for example, money transfer fees if you need your money in Norwegian Krone and the e-gold provider only pays out dollars.

Possibilities for use as digital currency
Would you like to spend your gold directly on other products instead of exchanging into national currency? If so then this could be useful, as more and more internet retailers are offering this as an option. Remember to investigate whether the fees are suited to the type of transactions you think you'll be making.

Advantages of Electronic Gold and Silver

- Internet-based, so a very accessible product with low costs
- Pooled investment, so secure storage costs are less than going it alone
- Your investment can be stored safely outside of local government jurisdiction
- Easy to buy and sell just by logging in to your PC
- Can be used as a medium of exchange in business transactions, and can even work out cheaper than bank conversion of national currencies

Disadvantages of Electronic Gold and Silver

- You are trusting a third party organisation with your wealth, so you need to be sure that they are definitely holding the relevant amount of gold to meet all their depositors. If a particular organisation ever gets into trouble, your gold and entire wealth could be at risk.
- Governments may target digital currency providers because they feel they are missing out on tax revenue or that their National currencies are being undermined. Ironically, the USA, long-regarded as the "land of the free", is currently leading the way in this respect. How this affects your savings is uncertain.
- Unlike credit card payments, payments with digital currency are usually irreversible. Most providers do make this major difference clear up front, so if there are any issues concerning a trans-

action, Eg. faulty or non-delivered goods, then it would be up to you to chase up the situation with whatever legal backing is necessary. EBay has banned the use of E-Gold and allegedly cancels any auction offering E-Gold as a payment method, although some critics claim that this is mainly done to protect their vested interest in Paypal, their own online payments system.

Before going any further, some readers may ask why the fact that electronic currency providers, unlike banks and bank deposits, aren't regulated or financially backed by the government in any way has not been listed as a major disadvantage. Well, to be honest, part of the attraction of gold is the independence of national borders and constraints that holding it should bring. Considering past histories of government mismanagement of national currencies and confiscation of wealth, who can you really truly trust to look after your hard-earned money?

The major people involved with the well-known digital currency businesses are all greatly enthusiastic about the subject of gold, 100% believe in gold as the one true store of value and often write articles displaying their depth of knowledge on the subject. So when it comes to trust, could you really consider them to be any less trustworthy than the average politician?

There are a lot of providers out there, but as a British citizen living in the European Union a lot of them were found to be heavily slanted towards the US market. For example, only accepting payment in dollars or paying out in dollars. One name that springs to mind as being of sound principle but US-based is "Liberty Dollar", as the name implies. Another is the Gold Dinar system based in the Middle East.

One more thing you will have to consider is the application criteria for your chosen provider. In order to meet with government money laundering regulations and the like, many providers require multiple copies of documents for proof of you and your address, and perhaps even notarised documents from your bank or lawyer. This can add extra administration, cost and time to opening an account.

We'll now cover some of the main providers that cater for citizens throughout the world and do not discriminate against non-US citizens, by which it is meant non-US citizens who otherwise might end up paying extra bank transfer fees, etc.

E-GOLD

E-Gold was one of the first organisations to offer this service. It was started up by a Dr Jackson who strongly believes in the gold story, and that gold is due a comeback as the trusted medium of exchange. E-gold started out in the USA and have since moved their jurisdiction to Nevis in the West Indies.

They offer deposit facilities and also heavily promote the use of e-gold for payments. There could be an exciting future for e-gold, but unfortunately, they are having to deal with various allegations made by the US Government, including aiding and abetting illegal activity and running an unregistered banking institution.

Some critics wonder whether the reason they are being chased is the alleged use of e-Gold for fraudulent purposes, or whether it is an attempt to stop US citizens from dumping the ailing dollar, placing their wealth outside of US jurisdiction and using a truly international hard currency.

The next important point is that e-Gold continues to operate as a legitimate business and is not being singled out by the US Government, as right now they seem to be chasing a lot of internet gold and silver providers including the aforementioned Liberty Dollar scheme. Any US citizen should probably be monitoring the actions of their government very carefully right now, as they seem to curtailing a lot of the principles attached to free movement of wealth, internet gambling being another example. As fair or unfair as this ongoing saga may be, if you are a US citizen you might want to consider your own intended usage of any digital currency provider because of government actions. Nobody can possibly predict future legislation and its effect on business dealings, least of all this book.

People conducting business on the internet may find an e-gold account especially useful because of its slant towards being used as a medium of exchange, and even traditional businesses in countries with high inflation could use it in future to agree prices with customers in terms of gold regardless of what happens to their national currency.

E-Gold have had such success with Gold, that they are now offering e-Silver, e-Platinum and e-Palladium too.

The process for transferring money into and out of E-Gold involves the use of separate payment providers. Authorised and recommended organisations are listed on their website. There is a fee of approximately 2% for transfer of funds in and transfer of funds out, plus you may also be liable to local bank fees. Different payment providers seem to have different fees, so it is well worth finding the best one for you. This system is quite flexible in that you can use a variety of payment systems to transfer money in or out, such as a credit card or Paypal account.

E-Gold also charge a storage fee for the days in which you own precious metals within their system. This is currently 1% per annum. This system of charging could work well for smaller amounts, or where your metal is used as a medium for exchange and thus many days your account holding is zero.

GOLDMONEY

This is the brainchild of highly-respected gold watcher James Turk. You pay a fee only when you buy, although this does seem to mean that the buy bid price is higher than some other alternatives.

Goldmoney has been structured with a cast iron guarantee that there will always be 100% gold backing of every unit of currency (called "goldgrams" in this case) in circulation, and they claim that some others such as E-gold and Perth Mint do not have the same cast-iron guarantees in their small print. Whether this is true or not is hard to say, as for an ordinary investor the small-print is difficult to understand, but the discussions and articles available make interesting reading when deciding on the safety of providers you are considering.

Goldmoney, like e-gold, also tries to offer the use of Goldmoney as a medium of payment. This however is not very heavily used right now, and the majority of investors are gold bugs simply buying gold and silver and holding it.

Monthly storage fees are also low. At time of writing, for gold, it is a flat 1/10 of a gram of gold per month, or about $2.43 per month. This is regardless of holding size, so is an extremely good deal for larger holdings that are not traded regularly.

If you are a US citizen, then you could find their regular savings "Gold Accumulation Plan" to be a winner. It works on the basis of the time-tested investing concept of unit cost averaging, where a fixed monthly amount saved buys x number of goldgrams at the spot rate + 1.9%. As the author is a British citizen, it is aggrieving that they don't yet offer this superb plan in other countries, as this is one of the best deals for investing in gold found anywhere. Enquiries indicate that this service may be in operation at some point in the future.

What could appeal to British or EU citizens about Goldmoney is that it is Jersey-based. You may trust and understand the rules of Jersey more than those of the Caribbean or Panama. This is not to say that other organisations are unsafe. A US-citizen may just as easily understand Panama and believe it to be much safer than Jersey.

GoldMoney recently introduced a Silver option, and this represents an excellent opportunity for European Union buyers to buy Silver bullion without legally paying any VAT. More latterly they also introduced the ability to hold the national currencies of Dollars, Pounds or Euros in your Goldmoney account and receive interest on it. You can then switch your holding between any of the five denominations (including the two metals), as you see fit.

Knowing that it's the fees that make investors poor and brokers rich, you are probably best off not utilising this feature. The fees will quickly eat into your returns, and a buy-and-hold strategy is probably best.

Payment into GoldMoney is by bank transfer. Payment out can be made by direct bank transfer and often these can be free of charge, for example if you live in the UK and receive your currency in Pounds to a British bank account using the UK BACs system. If your preferred currency is not Pounds, Dollars, Canadian Dollars or Euros, GoldMoney also offers the use of Payment Providers to help transfers into and from your chosen currency, although there may be other fees on top to consider.

One other aspect of GoldMoney worthy of mention is that if you account is not logged into for 12 years the ownership of your gold reverts to Goldmoney. Okay, it sounds unlikely, but consider what would happen if you died and never told anybody about your holding or even if you were unable to use the internet for 12 years due to some kind of accident or national crisis.

Overall, a highly respected organisation with the reputation of a known "gold-watcher" behind it. Even if you don't buy Goldmoney then Turk's articles are available for free on the website and make interesting reading.

BULLIONVAULT

Founded by Paul Tustain, BullionVault sits somewhere between Goldmoney, for safety and Gold storage, and the trading services mentioned earlier. Bullionvault is UK-based, although an additionally interesting feature is the ability to store your gold in their New York, London or Zurich gold vaults. Dependent on which country you are a citizen of, you will probably feel most comfortable placing your gold outside of that country so that is not subject to your local government jurisdiction, so top marks for considering that feature.

An interesting aspect of the three separate vaults is that these could be considered as separate currencies in their own right. For example, if at some point in the future there was a repeat of the 1930s US Gold confiscation, gold stored in a New York Vault might become priced significantly lower than gold stored in a Zurich vault, as US holders try to sell and place their gold outside their own jurisdiction.

BullionVault allows you to buy and sell Gold on their impressive looking trading platform, where buyers and sellers of gold from each vault can meet and state their required selling/buying prices, so if you are more in-clined to hold gold, occasionally sell on a dip, then buy in again later, then this could well be the best service for you.

Their fees for transactions and monthly storage are really low too, so they are very worthy of investigation. The storage fee is currently $4 per month fixed, regardless of holding size, and only payable for the months in which you held Gold.

Again, Bullionvault has proved popular with Gold Bugs accumulating gold for the future financial crisis they believe is in the offing.

Payment in to BullionVault is by bank transfer. Payment out is by bank wire transfer to your chosen bank account. A fee of approximately $30 is charged for this transfer, although there may be possibilities for UK residents to request a BACs transfer instead, which can take a few days but will not attract a fee.

There is no Silver option. This may be something to do with Bullion Vault being UK-based and the UK charging VAT on silver sales, which could, to many observers, seem to be another example of government getting in the way of free trade.

BullionVault are currently offering a free gram of gold to all new account openings, which you can then use to experiment with trading in their system. Even if you open an account, you are not committed in any way, so well worth trying out to see if it's for you. Visit http://www.investgold.co.uk to learn more.

OTHER WAYS TO INVEST

Okay, so new we've covered the major ways of investing in Gold and Silver, but can you think of any other ways that could pay off in the future?

One suggestion would be to consider buying Internet domain names with a precious metals angle. These could either be developed into relevant websites on the subject that generate cash using Google Advertisements and/or Affiliate Links, or just parked with a domain parking service in the hope of resale at a profit.

If you're not quite sure what I mean, check out . the two sites connected to this book:-

http://www.investgold.co.uk
http://www.investgold.eu

It is fair to assume that if there is ever a financial crisis and Gold and Silver once again come to the fore, then relevant domain names, especially those with traffic, could be worth a lot more, or be more cash generative than their yearly domain registration and web hosting fees are costing.

Should you wish to experiment with this route, then at the two websites listed above you will find some of the cheapest domain name registers that you can find and buy your domain names from.

There are probably many other ideas out there that have not even been thought of yet, but could prove to be spectacularly profitable. It justs needs your own creativity!

GOLD AND SILVER INVESTING SCAMS

It would be unwise to complete this book without warning you about some of the major scams being perpetrated today. The sad thing is that many of these scams use the worldwide reputation of value and wealth that precious metals, especially Gold, represent as a way to lure naïve investors into parting with their cash.

Firstly, never buy gold of uncertain value from unknown sources. This could include jewellery from street traders or even coins from internet auction sellers with no prior sales record. There is simply too much at risk to do otherwise, unless you really feel that the lower price you are paying justifies the risk. In most, if not all cases, it will not, so when buying physical gold, always buy from reputable, well-established sources with good feedback.

Secondly, if a deal looks too good to be true, it probably is. The price of gold in a variety of currencies is listed everywhere daily, so anyone with gold knows its approximate value, therefore why would they offer to sell it to you cheaply? Often people believe they have bought gold bars, later to find that they are lead inside, as lead is a similar weight. Again, to be safe here, only consider buying only from reputable sources where you can go for redress if anything goes wrong.

The internet, abounding with opportunities, whilst also fraught with dangers is the new wild west of the 21st century, and has also brought forth new avenues for criminals. One of the most common of these is a *Gold Investing scam*. These scammers play on the fact that people have heard about digital precious metal-backed currencies, but do not have much knowledge about how they really work. Many of these scammers can be found advertising on the right-hand side of the Google search engine in the Google-Ads section if you make a Gold-related search, making outlandish claims such as "make ½ to 5% per day" or "double your money in 30 days". If you are happy that your PC is protected against things like viruses and other worm software infecting it, then you could try visiting some of these sites to familiarise yourself with the type of cons being perpetrated. Furthermore, every click from Google costs these scammers money, and that can be no bad thing either. Google are blameless here, as their Adwords is an excellent service for legitimate businesses and individuals to reach their target audience and there is no way they could be considered accountable for the actions of a criminal minority.

After clicking on the ad, what you'll often then find is a credible-looking website, with heavy use of financial terms and acronyms such as HYIP (High Yield Investment Program), that don't really mean much, along with outlandish claims about how you will get rich by starting with a small sum, like, say $50. This is often backed up by some unintelligible diagram showing gold being routed between various parties and somehow ending up in your account. Even after reading it carefully, you usually still don't understand how the money is made, and searching around the site for real contact details such as a name, address or telephone number throw up very little, if anything relevant.

Please don't ever be conned by these websites or even dubious emails, often from places like Nigeria, offering you the chance to make instant, huge sums of money through gold, silver, digital currency or whatever. If it looks too good to be true, and you can't understand how it works, then it is most probably best to avoid it.

Truth is, if anyone can truly find an investment that returns even ½% per day, the best approach would be to keep quiet until you owned all the gold in the entire world, which, with compounding actually probably wouldn't take as long as you think!

The other sad thing is that E-gold is often the route for this illegally-earnt money because it's harder to trace and will cost too much money for the victims to take the perpetrators to court, assuming you ever even find out who the perpetrators are. E-gold are blameless, as they do make clear up front the irreversible nature of their payments system, but it may affect their credibility longer term, as many potential future users are put off by their lack of knowledge and bad first experience of the world of digital currency.

There are plenty of sites out there full of sad cases of people sharing with others their experiences of how their money has gone, with no replies and no money back. Given the fact that very few of us, if any, ever get the right financial training in our early years, including schooling, to prepare us for the serious financial decisions we'll have to make in our adult lives, is it a wonder so many naïve and trusting people can be conned by such schemes?

The overriding advice here is to only invest with reputable and well-established Gold sites.

Internet Auction Site Scams

While Internet auction sites are a highly recommended resource for buying many, many things, precious metals, especially Gold, are probably not among them.

When you are trading something like Gold, it is important to know you are buying from a reputable source, with comeback if anything is wrong with your purchase. Aside from this, you also have to consider postal costs and possible import duties on top.

If you ever do find yourself buying something from the likes of EBay, then follow a few simple guidelines. Make sure you pay using Paypal, and that your account is funded using a credit card. This gives you the most protection to get your money back if anything goes wrong with the transaction, such as the goods not turning up or being not as described.

Another scam to be aware of is when selling items of your own on EBay. EBay are mentioned here specifically, not because EBay is in any way a fraudulent site, but mainly because of it's major associations with its payment processing company, Paypal and the lack of understanding of how it works by sellers. Often buyers from strange countries far from your own will bid on your items and pay using Paypal. After a few weeks, they will register non-arrival of your item, even though you know you sent it and it most probably arrived fine. Under such circumstances, they will claim for, and eventually receive a refund from Paypal, and Paypal will then take the money back from you. Unless you took out adequate insurance on the item, which the buyer should pay for, and successfully claim for your loss from the Post Office then you are the loser. You are warned about this so you can make a clear decision about offering Paypal as a payment option when selling valuable items such as Gold coins.

SUMMARY

Traditionally, holding gold meant either Gold Coins or jewellery, stored either in your home or local bank, but the internet and electronic trading platforms on it have opened up a new world of Gold and Silver investing to the normal man on the street.

Many previously closed ways of investing in gold easily, such as share-dealing or futures trading are now available, but it has also spawned spread betting and the completely new concept of *digital currency*.

In the case of digital currency, the declining value of national currencies and rising worldwide internet access could see this new medium for storing wealth and facilitating trade come to the fore and we may yet only be in the early days of a new monetary paradigm.

Armed with the knowledge that these options are available, you should feel confident about investing in gold and silver in the ways that best suit your needs and at the lowest fees.

And now it's time to reiterate that this publication is not directly inducing you to invest or not invest in any particular product, merely to identify opportunities to invest more cheaply, so that more of your money remains your own and secondly to identify possible areas of precious metals investment that are unknown to the majority of investors yet offer great scope to diversify your portfolio and improve your returns.

Please remember to visit the website to check out all of the links in this publication and also find recommended reading, at:-

http://www.investgold.co.uk

ABOUT THE AUTHOR

As an ordinary man on the street who has always been interested in investing and saving as a means of saving for the future of his family, he stumbled upon a book in 2003 entitled "The Future of Money" which is interesting and stimulating in the way it describes what currencies truly are and the government interference that destroys true, fair and global trade as it should be. At that point his savings were all in cash or Mutual funds, as well as the main family home, which counts as property.

What becomes apparent when you read further into the subject is that there is one true currency sitting there in the background that has been in use for thousands of years and has outlived all national currencies ever invented. In fact, most national currencies only gain trust in the first place by being directly linked to the hard assets of gold and silver. It seems as though once this trust is ingrained in the minds of the nation and taken for granted then that is when the fabric of the system comes under threat. In 1931 Britain abolished its peg to gold (remember the gold sovereign has a face value of one Pound?), and since then the Pound has lost about 98% of its purchasing power. In the year he was born, 1971, the last recent link between the modern financial system and gold was removed when USA removed the $35=1oz gold standard and let its currency float freely, and now, at time of writing $705=1oz Gold. As ever, history is our best guide to the future, so perhaps the world financial system as it exists now is in a transitional phase. Maybe the next great nation, possibly China, will assume the mantle of the new Gold Standard nation? Or maybe the internet with its new digital currency will grow and encourage more and more of us into conducting more and more of our daily trade without borders in internationally-accepted hard currencies rather than heavily-taxed and controlled national currencies?

The important thing is to be prepared, and while it is not advocated that you are 100% invested in gold or silver, everyone should probably consider some exposure to gold and silver as protection against the uncertainty of the changing world we live in and the financial crises that may occur.

Finally, the statements in this document are based on his own research into investing in Gold and Silver and are not those of an acknowledged precious metals investing expert. As such, you may have some comments to make. If you email him at alan@investgold.co.uk, or through the blog investgold-uk.blogspot.com, he will happily discuss and update this publication where necessary. It is intended to update this publication to reflect new offerings in the world of gold and silver investing.

He wishes you every success with your future precious metals investments.

RECOMMENDED RESOURCES

The links contained within the book are repeated here for your benefit.

You can visit http://www.investgold.co.uk to connect directly to all of these links.

Recommended Books
"The Intelligent Investor"
A classic book, originally written in the 1930s by Benjamin Graham, who also happens to have been Warren Buffett's mentor at one point. Still as relevant now as it was back then. Full of sensible advice on investing, with no get-rich-quick promises.

"Hot Commodities"
Jim Rogers is a latter day investing genius. While his two other books, especially "Investment Biker", are recommended this is an insight into the bull market Jim believes is coming. So far, his predicitions about the commodity bull market have been spot on, as evidence by the rising costs of oil.

"Empire of Debt "
If you think the USA is still the world's greatest and richest superpower nation, then this book might bring you back to reality. The USA is in fact the world's biggest *debtor* nation, owning the rest of the world, especially Asia, billions and billions of dollars. Even Warren Buffett likens the USA to a farm, "…where bits are sold off every year and an ever bigger mortgage gets taken out on what is left…".

"The Coming Collapse of the Dollar"
Co-authored by James Turk, founder of Goldmoney and one of the major Gold investing experts in the world today. This book is direct and straight to the point in its explanations, and not in any way a plug for his Goldmoney product.

"The Future of Money"
Written by Bernard Litauer, who has worked in the currency markets for many years, including the introduction of the Euro. It is a look at what currencies truly are and what they represent. There are few, if any, specific references to Gold, making it a good way of understanding what currency represents in society.

Terms

When it comes to financial terms, as well as using any search engine, *Wikipedia* is a very useful explanation tool for novices. You can find it at:-

http://www.wikipedia.org

Fractional reserve banking
The accounting trick which allows more and more money to be created and added to our existing paper-based financial system.

Compounding
The key interest adding trick whereby you earn interest on your prior years' interest.

Unit cost averaging / dollar cost averaging
The system whereby saving small amounts regularly over a long period of time usually outperforms lump sum savings.

Gold Standard
This a monetary system where each unit of currency in existence is backed by a certain amount of Gold. It was in use by all the major nations up to the beginning of World War 1.

Links
Gold Anti-Trust Action Committee
www.gata.org

Silver Users Association
www.silverusersassociation.org

Selftrade
www.selftrade.co.uk

Perth Mint
www.perthmint.com.au

ETFSecurities
www.etfsecurities.com

E-gold
www.e-gold.com

BullionVault
www.bullionvault.com

GoldMoney
www.goldmoney.com

THE END

If you're a UK investor, then you'll know that you are fired at from all angles about how important it is save and invest for the future, then you hear about tax-free ISAs (Individual Savings Accounts) and how they are an unmissable tax-free opportunity to invest.

So the next step is to visit your bank or call a financial advisor, isn't it?

Sadly not. In the investing jungle you'll encounter financial advisors with salesman tactics or some new mis-selling scandal and even your bank manager is out hunting to get the biggest cut of your savings he possibly can for the bank and his own promotion prospects.

None of this is compatible with your own investment objectives and the only solution is to empower yourself to make your own investing decisions, which is where this book can help you.

You'll learn:-

• How a 10-minute trip to your bank can stop them quietly ripping you off.
• How financial advisors make money and why it's costing you.
• Why Isas are not as "tax-free" as you are repeatedly told.
• The hidden way to buy £1 worth of assets for 90p or less. Sometimes much less.
• How the government and banks collude to devalue your savings.
• How to invest in Property, Gold and Commodities through ISAs.

...and much, much more.

Even if you're not a UK investor, then most of the investments the book highlights are open to all, and the reality of how financial advisors make their money from you will sound all too familiar.

This book can easily end up saving you hundreds or even thousands of pounds and it can even be very refreshing to play the banks at their own game and see some salesman squirm as you use your new-found knowledge when they try to sell you something.

The book is available at http://www.Lulu.com, http://www.doityourselfisa.co.uk and all good on-line book retailers.

Printed in the United States
218650BV00004B/14/P